The Telesales Handbook

A practical guide to setting up and running your own telesales operation.

FASTPRINT PUBLISHING
PETERBOROUGH, ENGLAND

The Telesales Handbook

ISBN 978-184426-724-8

First published 2009 by
FASTPRINT PUBLISHING
Peterborough, England.

Printed by
www.printondemand-worldwide.com

Contents

Introduction

Before we go any further let me take a quick moment to tell you what led me to write this book and why you should consider even listening to me.

I started my career on the telephone several years ago, making calls for a company that sold mobility products. They would advertise in the sunday magazines and then when people called in to ask for a brochure we would say, "rather than send you a brochure I could arrange a free demonstration for you…" or something along those lines and we would then book a demo for them with one of the field reps. Those that didn't book would get a brochure and a follow up call a few days later to attempt to book them again and so it went on. I then moved to a large outsourcer and spent time there seeing how the big boys did it. Then another move, as an account manager for an office supplies company, with a mixture of cold calling and account management. I learnt a few tricks there, not least the fact that sales don't just happen, there's actually some effort involved!. From there into my first management role as a Telesales and Marketing Manager – an interview that lasted about five hours for a job I didn't think I would get!

Then came working for myself and the launch into consulting and a few years of headaches, proposals, networking and spinning several plates at once.

Since that time I have helped a first division football club increase season ticket sales, a national accident management company train a couple of hundred new staff, written a telephone selling skills course (a course that I was asked not to call a sales course!), doubled the sales of an outsourcer using the same amount of staff and numerous other set ups, training sessions and improvements to established teams.

I suppose the best way to describe what I do is to use the statement used by my mother when asked what I do for a living - “If you have a call centre and you want it to do better he can help you and if you want to have your own call centre he can make it for you” – laymans terms, but it pretty much covers it. A long time friend of mine jokes that I can be “dropped in any town in the UK and as long as I have my mobile phone I can create a call centre” a grand claim I’ll agree, but probably not too far from the truth, if you work in any industry for long enough you will gain the contacts you need.

I decided to write this book partly because I get asked all the time what I do and how I do it and partly because I just love the industry. If you’ve ever stood in the middle of a buzzing call centre you’ll know exactly what I mean and those of you who haven’t just don’t know what you’re missing!

Add to this the people who work in the call centres, a mix of people of all shapes and sizes, cultures, opinions and personalities it’s either a huge can of worms waiting to be opened or a great place to flourish I can’t always decide.

At the last count the industry employed something like 1 million of the country’s workforce and yet we are probably one of the least understood and respected industries, but the fact remains many businesses today have realised that the telephone, used properly, is a very cost effective selling tool.

Section One

The how and why.

There are basically two ways for a business to enter the telemarketing arena.

- Operate their own call centre/telesales team
- Engage an outsource operation

Neither one is better than the other, the one you choose is the one that suits your needs best. If you have the time, space and inclination for your own operation then you will have 'hands on' control and be able to, for want of a better phrase, touch it and see it.

If, however, you don't fancy that approach then an outsourcer may be the way forward for you and your business.

The difficulty in this decision is that your internal sales or customer service team can 'make or break' your business.
There is no doubt that the telephone used properly, even against today's multi media society, is a very effective way of doing business.

There are lots of different terms for using the telephone to conduct business and the one you favour depends on your opinion and what you will be doing.

Such terms as contact centre, call centre, telesales, telemarketing, internal sales are all commonplace and will generally operate in much the same way.

Call/contact centre tends to be used for a more multi media focussed operation – those that have blended call flow (inbound and outbound) alongside email and direct mail. Whereas the other terms are more often than not used to define the sales teams of SME's and are generally more outbound focussed.

The purpose of this book is to not only help you decide which option is best for your business but also when you've made that decision how to make sure you can set it up and run it so that it works for you.

It will also be a great reference for when you have been running your team for a while and want to keep things on track and make sure you're getting the best from them.

Let's look firstly at why we use telemarketing. The telephone can be used to cover a multitude of tasks

- Lead generation
- Database cleaning
- Product/Service launches
- Appointment making
- Brand awareness
- Business development
- Product/service sales

Of course, just because it's not on the above list that doesn't mean it's not being done, you could add others to this list

- Exhibition/Seminar booking
- Mailshot follow up
- Order confirmation/taking
- Helplines
- Charity donations

and the list goes on...

Section Two

The reasons why

Basically, if you have a lot of people you need to talk to be it inbound or outbound, and you have limited time to do it in, then the telephone is likely to be your best choice.

So what are the benefits of using the phone over other means of customer contact.

Fields sales teams – generally more expensive than telesales as they very often need company cars, laptops, mobile phones and in their defence they can't possibly speak to as many customers in any given working day compared to telephone based sales.

Direct mail – can seem expensive with small returns, although in my humble opinion what you will find will happen is that those that don't respond to a telephone call may well respond better to a mailshot.

E-commerce – a sign of the times, the difficulty is that despite there being a massive rise in people doing business online – just take a look at Amazon or Ebay – people still want to know that they pick up the phone and can speak to a real person.

Despite having spent the last few years working in the call centre industry, I still feel that the telephone alone is not enough in today's business world.

For example, following up a mailshot will generally reap bigger rewards that just cold calling.

Giving out a number to call when ordering online allows for operators to up/cross sell and increase revenue.

You can see, I'm sure, that working a couple of methods together very often gives the best results.

There are lots of things to consider when contemplating a telesales operation for your business, whether you pick an outsourcer or you choose to set up your own operation and I will do my best to help you 'get through it' whichever one you choose.

Ok, lets begin...

Why telesales etc.

The first thing you need to decide is why you think you need a telemarketing operation, where will they be based, what will they cost you, how many sales you'll need, what systems to use etc.

Ok, if your head is already hurting trying to decipher all that, don't worry. I'll separate it all out and we'll look at all the components separately, but firstly I'm going to give a summary of all the components and get into the detail later.

Right first things first, you need to decide what you want to use your operation for. As I mentioned earlier there are several ways in which a telephone operation can be used and very often the nature of your business or industry will, certainly in the initial stages, dictate what you use the telemarketing for.

For instance, if you currently use a field based sales team then you probably want to use the telesales team to book appointments for the field team. There are some important pointers we'll go over later that you will need to asses before they start calling.

If you just want to sell your product or service then we're talking about telesales in probably it's most purest form – more commonly known as cold calling. These are the most tenacious amongst telesales people. These are the one's who make 150 cold calls a day in the hope of getting a few sales. It's probably the hardest job to do in the industry, the hardest to recruit for, the hardest to keep doing and the one that will probably die out first.

Having spent an awful lot of time at the start of my career doing exactly this I know from bitter experience what it feels like. I think the phrase I'm probably looking for is "soul destroying" or in the words of one of my first bosses "a necessary evil!"

Now at the other end of the scale you have your customer service teams, those that have the dubious task of waiting for the customer to call to place an order or change their order or just complain.

I could probably go on all day about the different uses of a telesales operation, but that would be pointless, so we'll stop at the three I've just mentioned as they are probably the most common.

Right, let's assume we've now decided what we're going to use our team for. Next we have to look at how many of them we think we need.

Let's use the outbound stuff as an example, a straight forward telesales operation, calling businesses or consumers.

Now how many you want in your team is defined by a few things, not least how many sales you want to make. This then breaks down to a couple of other issues, how much is a sale worth to you, is it priced correctly, will people buy on the first call and what is your operator costing you etc. We can break most of that down into a very simple formula, known as cost per seat.

Allow me to explain, cost per seat works like this.

Firstly you need to know how much an operator costs you, meaning if they sit there all day and make no sales you still have to pay the wages etc, so what is that cost...

Hourly wage (£7.00 p/h)

+

Hourly cost of calls (telephone bill, let's estimate £2.00 p/h)

+

Utilities cost (electric etc, again we'll work with £2.00 p/h)

This covers the cost of your operator, so using the above figures, each 8 hour day, they cost you £88.00 per day or £440.00 per week or £1760.00 per month (obviously these are approximate figures but they will do for the sake of this calculation)

Forgive me if this next bit seems obvious, but this is what happens, each operator costs you £88.00 per day, if each sale is worth £22.00 to you they have to make 4 sales each day just to get you to break even.

Now we can expand on this, if a sales is worth £200.00 to you they are much more likely to have less sales per day, but it doesn't matter because they're still covering their costs and to be perfectly honest you'll probably only make one sale a day due to the cost to the customer, but again at £440.00 a week cost, three sales a week would still be ok for covering costs, although you will probably want to question the skills/motivation of that particular agent – more on that later.

Now, break even is all good and well but I'm assuming you're not doing this just to cover your costs, I'm guessing you want to make some profit amongst all this.

So now we're talking about targets...

We'll go back to our original cost of £88.00 per day with a sale value of £22.00.

Four sales a day pays the bills, so what you need to do is set them a target of 8 (one an hour) giving you £176.00 per day meaning after costs you still make £88.00 per day, per agent.

More about targets and target setting later.

I'll just quickly cover systems and then we can start getting into the nitty gritty of what you need to do and how to do it.

Systems basically covers the things you'll need to physically make the calls, record them etc.

If you intend to have just a small team then an excel spreadsheet will probably suffice in recording data etc, if you're going bigger then you may want to consider a CRM system or Customer Relationship Management system. These are generally software based systems that can do all sorts of great stuff for you, as before we'll get into those in more detail later on.

Hopefully this has started to give you an idea of what's involved in setting up and operating any sort of telephone sales operation. I'm sure your head is probably spinning for the moment, but please don't worry, by the time we've got to the end of this handbook you'll be more than prepared to do everything you need to do, whether you decide to opt for your own outbound operation or go with an outsourcer.

What I'll do throughout the rest of this guide is talk as if you're setting up your own operation and then make comparisons as if you we're opting for an outsourcer.

I'm also going to use the term telesales to make things easy, you can just substitute this for whichever team you're going for.

Section Three

Setting up your telesales team

Again, for the sake of making things easy, we'll assume we're setting up a team of ten agents, making outbound calls.

Although the same principals will generally apply with whatever type of team you're setting up.

We've already talked about your cost per seat, so let's assume that we've decided on ten agents because it fits our budget and brings us the amount of sales we want/need.

Remember the cost per seat formula is

Hourly wage (£7.00 p/h)
+
Hourly cost of calls (telephone bill, let's estimate £2.00 p/h)
+
Utilities cost (electric etc, we'll work with £2.00 p/h)

This covers the cost of your operator, so using the above figures, each 8 hour day, they cost you £88.00 per day or £440.00 per week or £1760.00 per month (obviously these are approximate figures but they will do for the sake of this calculation)

Each operator costs you £88.00 per day, each sale is worth £22.00 to you so they have to make 4 sales each day just to get you to break even.

Four sales a day pays the bills, so what you need to do is set them a target of 8 (one an hour) giving you £176.00 per day meaning after costs you still make £88.00 per day, per operator.

Of course, if you have to add anything else into the cost per seat formula – postage to send out catalogues etc - it will change, but all it will do is increase the amount which will mean your team will have more sales to reach break even.

With ten agents in your team, you're obviously going to need, ten desks, ten chairs, ten telephones, probably ten PC's and I would suggest ten headsets.

First things first, you'll need to make sure you have the room for that – when you do this you need to consider not just the size of the desks (there are health and safety issues there) but also storage and some room to move.

Presuming you have we can move on to the next stage.

Recruitment

Basically, for it to run smoothly you will need to have a team with a structure, with someone to take the helm. Even if they report to you, you'll still need to have someone who's responsible for the day to day running of the operation.

If you don't already have a sales manager you're probably going to need someone who's role is to oversee the team, set their targets, make sure they reach them, conduct appraisals etc.

Now I appreciate that I'm waffling on again and I promise we will cover all of this stuff as we work through the process, so please don't panic, I just need you to understand how involved this is at the beginning – but it does get easier, that I can assure you.

Right, so we've organised the basics and we now have a room in the building dedicated to our telesales team. Now we need to look at getting your staffing needs.

When you recruit your ten agents you'll need to be thinking about someone to oversee the daily operations as I mentioned earlier.

A process that has worked very well for me over the years is to recruit your ten agents and at interview stage you tell them that there is an opportunity to gain promotion to a team leaders position but don't pick someone straight away.

What you'll find will happen is as the agents go through their training one or more of them will naturally take the lead and these are the ones from which you choose your first team leader.

Recruitment for a telesales team can be difficult if you're new to it. You have a couple of choices when starting out.

- Making your own efforts

- Using a recruitment agency

I would suggest a mixture of both to get you started. Using a recruitment agency is a quick fix as they generally have several people already on their books who would fit your needs, but it will cost you a little more in the beginning.

If you do use an agency, make sure they come and see you, where the agents will be working and allow you to discuss in detail what you expect from the agents. You're far better off giving them a job spec at the beginning and asking for exactly what you want, firstly to save yourself any wasted interview time and secondly, it's their job to find you what you want, that's what they get paid for, doing all the leg work for you.

When organising your own recruitment campaign you have several options you can follow.

- Local paper adverts
- The job Centre

- Free online classified websites
- Flyers
- Word of mouth

All of these have given me some success in the past, again I would suggest using as many of them as you can so that you have plenty of people to choose from, so that you get the best possible team right from the start.

Let's have a quick look at each one,

Local paper adverts
Depending on your budget, a simple lineage advert will normally be enough, you can be fairly cryptic with the wording you use, firstly because you're likely to be paying by the word and secondly, you want to tease the applicants not tell them everything upfront.

Such as,

*Experienced telesales agents required for a exciting new project, excellent ote and promotion prospects for the right person. Phone 0*** 9** **** for more info.*

These sorts of adverts will generally bring in plenty of response, I would suggest you take the contact details of any callers – name , number and any experience – and tell them you will call them back.

What this does is put the control of the call with you not them, give them a time when you will call so you can see how they answer the phone and how keen they are – if they really want the job they'll make sure they are in a quiet place to take your call.

We'll go through some sample questions to ask at the end of this section.

The Job Centre
I've personally had limited success using this method but I have colleagues who have found exactly the person they where looking for.

You can give lots of information about the role and your company and it will cost you nothing!

It will get put on their website and can be searched from all the Job Centre job points.

Free Online Classifieds websites
These are like the job centre as regards cost, nothing, which in my opinion is always a good price, *if* it brings the results you want.

The one I've used most often is www.gumtree.com they have lots of the main cities of the UK already covered and are bringing in more all the time.

Placing an advert is relatively easy and you can put lots of information about want you're looking for etc with no cost attached.

The downside can be that the adverts only last for a few days and can 'move down the line' as the week progresses, although on some sites you can pay a few pounds to keep it at the top if you wish

I wouldn't panic too much about this though, I've placed adverts for clients and had responses a month later, people do take the time to look at these sorts of sites because they cover a lot more than just jobs.

Flyers
This one is really simple and works best if your in a busy part of town, or near a university etc.

All you do is design a really simple, catchy flyer. Take a handful of them, walk outside and hand them out to likely candidates, simple, effective and fairly cheap to do.

Word of mouth
Firstly, if you have any, tell your current employees what you're going to do and offer them an incentive to tell their friends – vouchers or money is always a good one – and if the person they refer stays a set period of time, say three months, then they get a reward.

Secondly, when you've started to recruit some agents tell them the same thing. Most people who have worked in the environment for any length of time get to know others that do.

Now let's talk about the interview process and the sort of questions you need to be asking.

If you're recruiting for an outbound telesales team then you want to recruit agents with experience in that area. That may sound a little obvious, so let me expand. People who work in the outbound environment do so because they have the skills and because they enjoy it, now this is a generalisation, but those that have a customer service or inbound background rarely make a successful change to outbound.

Working in outbound requires you to be very tenacious, to be thick skinned and to be able to accept lots of no's before you get that much sought after yes.

So when you call back the people you've chosen in the early stages firstly ask them to expand on their experience. What you're looking for is people who have experience that matches what you think your agents need. You may not find exact matches but your looking for similarities rather than the perfect agent.

Things like, you want them to make calls business to business but all their experience is business to consumer. Not a complete catastrophe but you'd need to dig a bit deeper into what they were selling and the cost and see how it compares to your own product/service.

How long have they been working in telesales, how and why did they get into it and what are their career plans. Your looking for longevity, you don't want someone who's had six telesales jobs in the last year – they're either not very good, they don't tend to stick at anything or they're hard to manage.

If you told them your company name when you first spoke to them, which you no doubt did, then ask them what they know about you. If they want to work for you not just any telesales job then they should have a least tried to find out what you do.

Following this ask them why they want to work for you and what they expect from it.

Once you've had this brief chat with them, if you're still happy and want to interview them face to face, ask them to send in a CV and tell them you'll be interviewing next week and you will contact them should you wish to invite them in.

I would suggest that whether you want to interview them or not it is only polite and professional that you let them know.

Take some notes when you're doing the phone interview and then when the CV arrives compare it to your notes to make sure it's the same. People will lie on their CV, nobody minds the odd wrong date etc but you don't want your notes to look like it's from a totally different CV.

Once you've picked your interview candidates, you'll need to arrange the first interviews.

I would suggest a two part interview. First interview to be conducted by yourself, the Sales Manager or the HR manager, just one person is fine for this stage and the second interview to be conducted by whoever did the first interview and one other person. This way you get two different opinions of the candidate. This is always useful because on the second interview the 'other' person can very often see things that the first person didn't, not because they are any better at interviews, but because they'll have a different viewpoint on some aspects and you can compare notes.

Remember, an interview is where a candidate tells you why they are the best person for the job. It's up to them to convince you not for you to sell the company to them. Remember, they want to work for you.

There are lots of books and websites that will give you plenty of tips and questions for interviews but generally this sort of thing works well and will give you a good idea of the sort of person in front of you.

What do you know about us?

Why did you apply for the role?

Are you working at the moment?

Give me three things your current/last employer would say about you.

Why did you/do you want to leave your last/current role?

What are your strengths/weaknesses?

What can you bring to the role?

Where do you see yourself in 5 years?

These are just a base to work from, you will find that their answers will prompt you to ask more questions.

What you also need to look for and I'll apologise now if you've conducted interviews before but this is one of my pet hates when it comes to recruiting.

They should be on time, preferably a few minutes early and they should be dressed accordingly – suit & tie etc – I regret to say that I have turned people away from interviews due to them rolling up in jeans etc. You may think this is a little harsh but here's my thinking. They've come to you for an interview because they want the job you're offering. If they can't even be bothered to 'dress to impress' – first impressions do count – then how will they approach the job and your customers?

When you've got your ten people, let them know by letter, even if you call them to offer the role first and make sure that you have a contract to give them the day they start.

I would also suggest that you put together a staff handbook which outlines the does and don't for the team. Things like dress codes, fire drill, personal calls and the like. It just let's everyone know exactly where they stand right from the start.

Of course, if you decide to use an agency they will do most of the legwork we've just talked about for you. It may take you a few CV's before the agency work out what you're looking for but then all you have to do is conduct the interviews.

As I mentioned, doing it this way does cost a little extra to do, especially in the first few weeks but it will give you a bit more control when people turn out to be not what you expected. You just call the agency and get them to deal with it.

The other thing to consider is that after a set period most agencies will let you take the agent on as a full time employee, very often at no cost.

When setting up a call centre, acquiring the right staff is imperative to maintaining your good reputation.

To make sure you are filling your call centre with the best possible people, a strict recruitment process is crucial. Seeking the assistance of an agency can save you time, money and effort, meaning by the time you meet with candidates they are already at second interview stage. Whether you are using an agency, or recruiting yourself, a detailed job description and person specification is needed to gain the appropriate staff, as all call centres require different skills, depending for instance on inbound or outbound needs.

We have found that one of the best recruitment processes when finding call centre staff is dedicated assessment days, incorporating role plays, competency based interviews and personality tests.

It is sometimes necessary to look beyond a CV, as someone might have the necessary skills but perhaps not the right background; this is where an agency can assist in delivering you with a shortlist from the available applicants.
Whichever route you choose when recruiting for your call centre, remember - your business can only ever

be as good as the people who work for you – Sarah Dineen, Meridian Business Support,

For more information you can contact Sarah at sdineen@meridianbs.co.uk

---

Facilities

A phrase that covers everything from light bulbs to toilet rolls, but in our case it covers desks, chairs, PC's, telephones, headsets etc.

Desks
They need to be the right shape and size and fit with health and safety, which if I remember correctly means 1000mm from front to back – but please check for yourself in case it's changed since the writing of this guide – and accommodate what they'll need.

For example if they need to have a PC a telephone and three letter trays they I would suggest either a radial desk (a corner desk to you and me) or something nice and long.

Chairs
My suggestion, as a minimum, would be for a high backed operators chair. They come with removable arms and they can be adjusted to fit the individuals needs – don't forget to conduct a work station review before the team starts.

PC's
This is a personal choice, but as long as they have the capacity to cope with the workload and software you require, it's up to you what you spend and which make you choose.

Telephones
Again it really depends on what you want them to do. Whether you just want them making outbound calls or whether you want them to be able to make outbound calls and accept incoming calls or if they're going to be totally customer service.

The best advice I can give you is to think about what you want them to do and then speak to some suppliers. There's plenty of them out there and if you speak to a few you can play them off each other to get the best deal.

Headsets

This really depends on whether you want your team to use them. They're not particularly expensive in the grand scheme of things and if your team are going to be using PC's etc then they can be very useful and generally make the team more efficient and productive.

You can get monaural (one ear piece) or binaural (two ear pieces) – which you chose is a personal choice - some phone systems suppliers often offer them as part of the deal.

All of this will certainly make your team operational, anything else you want to add is down to your own preference. Although I would strongly suggest you think about the environment they'll be working in, so maybe stick in some nice pictures or plants in the room.

We'll talk about this more later in the book, but for now just bear it in mind.

Script

Ok, so we have a team, somewhere to put them and the tools they need to do the job.

So they need to know what to say.

The script is a very important part of what your team is going to need. I would suggest that they don't read it off a piece of paper for their whole career with you, but they will have to at the beginning – but then with regular training and lots of practice they'll use is as a reminder and nothing else.

What you need to remember when writing your script is that what works face to face is unlikely to work over the phone.

Look at it like this, if your sales rep knocks on someone's office door (doesn't happen very often anymore but bear with me) in their nice clean suit looking all presentable, then people are likely to at least let them say there first little bit. If you offer your hand to someone they are unlikely not to shake it. What your rep can also do at this stage is see how busy the prospect is, what mood they're in etc and make a judgement on their next action from what they see.

Now look at this from a telesales point of view. You telephone someone and if they take your call you have between 5 and 10 seconds to judge all the things that a face to face appointment can see instantly and the only way you can do this is to say something that the prospect wants to hear and their reaction to this will allow you to judge if you go on or not.

So with this in mind, the script needs to be short and to the point, at least with the introduction.

You'll need to state your name, the company and the reason for your call

You need to cover the things the customer wants to know (you'll know what these are as you're talking about your business). You'll need to be aware of the likely objections your going to get and have the answers and you'll need to have a couple of closes in there for good measure.

Now the last comments are based on an outbound call, as we've said before if you have an inbound team, then apart from the way you answer the call your script will be almost dictated by the customer – if they want to buy or they have a query etc – although you will no doubt have some prepared answers to standard questions and queries.

Once you've got a script that you're happy with you need to test it.

I can pretty much promise you the first version you write will not be the version you use. It will get changed and tweaked as time goes on. The one thing you should remember to do is constantly be looking to improve it – that's a job taken by the person who handles the day to day running of the team.

The best suggestion I can give you regarding your script is the sooner your team can perform it without reading it the better they will sound, the more confident they will be, which will lead to more sales.

It's one of those things that should be practiced constantly, day after day – how many times have we all received a telesales call and you ask a question out of the order they expected and it throws the whole thing off.

Now we've gone over a lot of stuff so far and there's more to come, but before we do let's just look at how the things we've covered so far compare to using an outsourcer.

We've covered where the team will go, recruitment, facilities, cost per seat and the script.

As regards where the team will sit, not your problem with an outsourcer, if they want your business it's up to them to create a team and put them somewhere.

Which leads us to the facilities, again not your problem. What I would suggest is that you visit their operation, don't take their word for how great it is and how happy their team are etc. Ask for a meeting at their premises. If you're going to put the success of your business in their hands you don't want to have any doubts at all about what's going to happen. Ask them how they prepare for a new contract, what training do the agents get, will they write a script, who will supply the data.

Cost per seat will again not be your problem, that's for them to worry about.

Basically it works like this, you tell them what you want, they give you an hourly rate and if you're happy with it then they have a new campaign to organise.

For you, as the client, using an outsourcer means an 'arms length' approach. You'll be reliant on what they do, it's unlikely they'll let you spend too much time onsite (and to be honest if you want to do that you may as well set up your own team).

You may have some involvement in the initial training of the team but will unlikely be involved in the ongoing process.

What will happen is that you and the outsourcer will agree a reporting schedule and that is probably the only contact you'll have with them. That isn't a dig at outsourcers, I have worked for and with several over the years and if you want to just let someone else crack on with the job while you reap the benefits then it's the ideal answer for you.

Remember to measure the success of any campaign – I'll show you how later in the book.

So to carry on from where we left off, we have recruited our team, we've got them somewhere nice to sit and a phone and PC to use and we've written a script now we need to train them how to use it all.

Training

The type of training your team gets is dependant on what they'll be doing but we'll stick with our outbound team scenario for the moment.

Remembering that we've recruited people with some experience of telephone sales and if you're lucky some experience of your industry, but you'll still need to cover some product/service training.

How involved that is and how long that will take is down to how complicated your product or service is, which will dictate to you how long you spend on this part of their training.

I would suggest starting with the basics of telephone sales, if you don't feel confident of doing this yourself there are people who can do it for you although I would suggest you look for a company who at the very least specialises in sales training, but ideally someone who trains specifically for call centres and telesales operations.

They should cover things like

- Preparing for the call
- Call structure
- Features and benefits

- Open and closed questions
- Objection handling
- Closing techniques

There's more they can do, for example if your team are calling business to business then they'll want some training on 'getting past the gatekeeper' – basically the receptionist or pa – a very important skill for the team.

If you're creating or using a customer service or inbound team then things like customer interaction and listening skills should be highlighted.

They'll also need some training on the correct useage of the phone system you'll be using – nothing worse for a customer than their call being cut off rather than transferred.

You also need to take into account how you expect them to conduct themselves when they're on the phone – remember they're representing you when they do it.

You will most definitely need to put into place some sort of training program so that they are kept up to speed with industry changes etc but that can be organised and delivered by your team manager as a part of their role.

Again to quickly mention the outsourcer option. If that's the way you've chosen to go then ask them what training they do for the agents, do they have a dedicated training team and do the agents just train for specific campaigns or do they train towards NVQ's or similar.

That done we now have a trained up team of agents with most of what they need to get on with the job

Now they need someone to call...

Data

If you've been in business for any length of time you'll have a customer database. Depending on what your business does it will be people who have ordered from you in the past or people who order from you month after month or a mixture of the two. You'll have the best knowledge of this but one thing I would say is everyone needs new business. Another one of those obvious statements I know but nine times out of ten a telesales team is used to create new business. So if we take this as our reason for creating the team let's look at their data needs.

First things first, are they calling businesses or consumers?

You'll have an immediate answer to this, but it will probably dictate what you pay for the data. Data is normally sold on a per record basis and the more specialised the data the more it's going to cost you.

If you just want homeowners, in a certain area it'll be fairly reasonably priced but as I said, the more specific you get the higher the price.

Next you need to decide how you want your data supplied to you.

Normally it's supplied as a CSV file (comma separated version) which is pretty much an excel spreadsheet. This sort of file will drop into most CRM systems. But if you have a specific type pf CRM system or want it done in a particular way then it's best to speak to a database company.

Remember though, that they are in the business of selling data, so they are normally fairly happy to help where they can and I would always suggest talking to two or three different suppliers.

Ensure the data you use is screened against the Telephone Preference Service. Ignoring this can result pretty hefty fines.

There is no substitute for in-house research. Always ask a potential data supplier how they collect their data. If they are vague or unable to give an answer, steer clear!

What to look for in a data supplier: They have as much communication with each contact on their database as possible. Generally speaking, telephone research is at the top with maximum contact (and therefore accuracy) and web harvesting is at the bottom with minimum contact.

Always ask a data supplier what quality guarantees they have in place, it can be used to judge the confidence they have in their own product!

Always keep a note of when the data has been inaccurate or out-of-date. A good supplier should refund these records for you. – Justin Elliott, Corpdata.

For further info you can contact Justin at Justin.Elliott@corpdata.co.uk

---

The other option you have, as I mentioned earlier, is using your own database if you have one.

I remember a conversation with a client that went something like this.

"How many customers do you have?"

"About 19,000 on the database"

"Great, how many of those buy from you each month?"

"About 11,000"

"So you actually have 11,000 customers"
"No we have 19,000"

"Yes but only 11,000 of those 19,000 spend money with you, so you've actually got 11,000 customers and 8,000 extra mailshot letters"

"Oh, I see what you mean…so what do we do with them?"

“I would suggest you get the guys in customer service to give the 8,000 a call and ask them why they don’t buy from you any more. When you have the reason you may be able to fix it and then they would be spending customers again”

“I like that idea, let’s do that”

That was the point where I then spent three weeks with their customers service guys sorting out that issue for them and they ended up with an increased database of spending customers.

All ego’s aside you can, I’m sure, see where I’m going with this. If you speak to your customers on a regular basis you will get more from them, just be careful not to go to far the other way and bombard them with calls, the personal touch is always good, but put a limit on it.

If you’re lucky you’ll be able to get a mixture of new business from your existing customers and from the data you bought.

One thing you must remember to do is record the activity so that you know how well it worked. I’m going to talk about that more in a bit but first I want to spend some time on calling hours.

Before we go any further I feel the need to mention The Data Protection Act. There are lots of different things in this act that have an affect on those of us using the telephone to make a living.

Firstly, there are very specific rules on how and where you keep data on customers and also what you write about those customers. Remember, if you hold details on a person they are within their rights to ask to see it.

Secondly, there are very specific rules on how you check the details of the person you're talking to, who confirms what etc.

The best thing to do is that while you're setting up your operation you must take into consideration, definitely the two points I just mentioned, but for your own safety and peace of mind check with the right people where you stand in regards to the calling activity you'll be undertaking. You need to be aware of any compliance issues.

The best thing to do is check with The Information Commissioners Office (ICO) then there will be no doubts.

www.ico.gov.uk

Calling Hours

As the name suggests this is the time your team spend on the telephone talking to customers and prospects.

There is a big difference between calling business to business and calling business to consumer.

The thing to remember is when is my customer or prospective customer going to be most receptive to my call.

Whether you have built your own team or whether you have decided to use an outsourcer the same rules will apply.

Let's take business to business first. We'll work on a 9 to 5 working day Monday to Friday.

Think about how your own working week pans out.

Would you happily accept a telesales call first thing on Monday morning?

If we're at all honest then the answer is probably going to be a no.

Also if we presume a lunch break for most people of 1:00pm – 2:00pm then why get your team to try and call people then, they'll be on lunch and you're wasting your time. The same thing works from about 4:30pm, people are starting to close down for the day.

Think about the same problem on Monday morning when you're calling on Friday afternoon.

I will be the first to admit that this is a generalisation and I have myself had successful calls at all times of the working day, but you need to be aware of these issues and act accordingly.

For example, if Monday mornings are going to be low on sales then why not have a regular sales/training meeting then. It will stop the agents getting frustrated and will allow you and the team manager to give them a motivational boost at the start of the week.

If possible give them the same lunch break as the rest of the working world – obviously if the people in the industry you're calling finish at 4:00pm everyday and therefore take lunch a midday you just adjust how your team approach it.

Why not have an end of week sales/reward meeting on Friday afternoons?

It again gets the team away from the frustrating times and allows you to see first hand how the week has gone, who's done well and to reward them etc. Business to consumer is slightly different but still has it's pitfalls.

Because you're likely to have them calling into the early evening then they will be starting later than their business to business counterparts.

Let's work with a 1:00pm to 8:00pm day. When planning your team lunch breaks, training sessions, sales meetings etc consider this.

Between 2:30pm and 3:30pm is school run time so your amount of connected calls is likely to reduce.

Around 5:00pm to 6:30pm is dinner/tea time and then at about 7:00pm the soaps start!

This is not meant to put you off from phoning consumers is there to allow you to plan your teams day to best effect.

If you're phoning prospective customers then I wouldn't advise calling past 8:00pm – this is, of course, just my opinion – but if you're calling your own customers then you can probably go as late as 9:00pm

The best way to look at it is this. You want to get the most out of every hour worked, so you need to plan your teams day so that they are on the phone as much as possible and gaining the best results. Just plan your teams day so that they get the best from it and stay motivated.

With the team in mind let's take a moment to look at the team structure.

We have a team of ten agents all working on the phones day in day out. You'll need someone to run the day to day activity, your team leader or team manager or whatever title you decide to give them.

Even if you already have a sales manager they're going to have other things to worry about so you'll still need someone to handle the day to day stuff.

If you recruit someone especially for this role then they need to have more experience that the rest of the team and hopefully have some relevant experience in running a team.

If you use my usual approach and recruit the team and see who takes the lead then will need to be the one who is always on time, asks loads of questions and helps the others without needing to be asked.

They will need to be able to plan the day and week for the team, set them targets and motivate them. They should also be prepared to take the phone if an agent is struggling or dealing with an irate customer/prospect.

They will also need to conduct regular team meetings and appraisals and be able to compile reports to show the teams performance etc.

I will show you how to do these things later on in the book but for now let's stay with setting up your team and getting them calling.

By now you should be pretty happy and confident in your new telesales operation and be waiting with bated breath for the first sale to come in.

Before we get on to the operation of the team and how to keep them motivated and performing at their best let's just check we've done everything.

- ❑ Have you worked out the cost per seat?
- ❑ Do you have space for them
- ❑ Have you organised the facilities – desks, chairs, phones etc?

- ❑ Have you decided on the calling hours?
- ❑ Have you decided on how you will recruit your team?
- ❑ Have you recruited your team and found a team manager?
- ❑ Have you got the data for them to call?
- ❑ Have you written the script they'll use?
- ❑ Have you given them the training they'll need?
- ❑ Have you set then their targets?

This done you're ready to let them loose and think about how you keep the team operating properly, efficiently and for the long term.

Section Four

Operating your team

There's a few things you need to be aware of when keeping your team operational.

First and foremost you need to set some boundaries. Salespeople, by their very nature, are the sort of people who if you give them an inch they'll take a mile (and sell it to someone!) so you need to establish the 'ground rules' right from the start.

That's why, if you remember, I suggested putting together a staff handbook and giving them a copy on their first day. That way there's no confusion and everyone knows where they stand.

It doesn't have to be huge and over complicated, they need to know their working day but they also need to know what you expect from them (everything else would be covered in their contract of employment)

Then you need to think about setting them some targets.

Setting the targets for the team is worked from a couple of different angles.

Firstly, you've already worked out cost per seat. You know what it's going to cost you for them to take up space in the office so that dictates your minimum cost.

Then you have to think about how many calls they can sensibly make in the working day and from there establish how many decision makers they will speak to within that amount and then how many sales they will get from that.

We can argue all day about the facts and figures on this, the fact remains that every industry will have it's own. It's likely that as you're working in the industry you're going to have a pretty good idea of what's achievable and that will allow you to make your decision on targets.

Secondly the cost of each sale. If what your asking the customer to part with is only a few pounds then you're likely to get a sale over the phone on the first call so your agents should be able to make several sales a day. Whereas if what you're asking for is a few hundred or even a few thousand pounds then it's going to take you a few calls per customer before you get the sale, so three or four a week might suffice, but always remember your cost per seat. If an agent isn't making enough sales to cover that then you have a decision to make.

So you need to think long and hard about these things before setting a target for the team – remember if you set the team a target of 100 sales per week, you have to divide that by nine for your team of ten because your team manager won't have much time on the phone so you're relying on the agents making the calls, so this will mean 12 sales each per week (it's actually 11.11 but we'll round it upwards to make sure) which means 2.5 sales each per day, per agent.

What you don't want to do is make the target too easy to reach or on the flip side of the coin make it too hard.

Too easy means they'll get lazy and complacent, too hard means they'll struggle to reach it and then get frustrated and possibly leave, so setting it at the right level is very important.

Try using the SMART process as a way to decide if the targets are where and what they should be.

It works like this...

S - specific,

M - measurable,

A - achievable,

R - realistic,

T - time-based,

You'll probably find slightly different variations of this if you search the internet but it all boils down to the same thing.

The target you set has to be **specific** (just sell more isn't really going to help anyone - 9 is more than 8 but won't really impress anyone)

The target has to be **measurable**, give them a figure against what they're currently doing.

It has to be **achievable**. Telling an agent who currently does 2 sales a day that you want them to do 10 a day as of tomorrow is probably going to end in that agent leaving. It's much better to ask that agent that you want them to eventually sell 10 a day but you'd like them to start by getting 4 a day this week and then 5 a day next week etc. Giving them a target that unachievable will just demoralise them which actually has the reverse affect.

Making the target **realistic** follows the same principal as making them achievable. If the target is realistic then the agent or team is more likely to try and achieve it, giving you the desired result.

And last but no means least, the target has to be **time based**. Don't just tell them to make more sales – although that's what you want – tell them how many more sales you'd like them to make – taking in to consideration the things we've just covered – and then give them a time scale to achieve it.

Of course, you can use this same target setting process if you decided to use an outsourcer. Don't let them set the target for you. Your the client, you've done your calculations so presuming you've been sensible with your target they shouldn't argue too much, they'll be working it out pretty much the same way we just have.

Now, the setting of your targets leads us to the next topic – Key Performance Indicators (KPI's)

Key Performance Indicators are what you use to record your teams targets, their performance and their ability to meet those targets.

Using our team of ten as an example you could quite easily use an excel spreadsheet. They're quite easy to produce as you won't need anything fantastic. The headings you use will depend on what you want to know but let me give you some idea of what I look for from a sales team

- Hours worked
- Calls (dials) made
- DMC (Decision Maker Contacted)
- NI (Not Interested)
- C/B (Call backs)
- Sales

You would have these listed for each agent and from these you can start looking into their conversions.

Again it's up to you what you want to find out but try these ,

- Dials to hours (how many dials they make per hour)

- Dials to DMC (How many dials they make to speak to a decision maker)

- DMC to sale (How many decision makers they have to speak to before they get a sale)

I'll apologise if this seems like I'm stating the obvious but allow me to expand on these a bit.

Dials to hours
You need to know how many dials (or calls) they make in an hour so you can look at the most basic state of their performance.

If you've got several agents at the same level - let's use 12 per hour – and then you've got one agent only making 8 an hour you could have a couple of reasons.

1. They're basically being lazy and not working at the same speed as the rest of the team

2. They're spending more time on the phone talking to prospects than everyone else – not necessarily a bad thing, you need to check their sales conversions to really decide.

3. They're struggling with their product knowledge or delivery of the sales pitch – which is a training issue.

Which of these it turns out to be you'll know when you talk to them and you can act accordingly.

Dials to DMC (Decision Maker Contacts)
Basically, how many calls they each have to make before they get to speak to the person they want to, the decision maker.

When you know this you'll be able to start judging the expected performance for new sales people and also how each day will pan out.

For example if you know that each person will make approximately 100 calls a day and that they will speak to 20 decision makers then you know that if you've got all nine of your agents on the phone for a day, between them they're going to speak to 180 decision makers that day.

Again if you've got a particular agent who's performing under your team average, you've probably got someone who's struggling to get past the gatekeeper (receptionist/PA) and therefore not getting to the decision maker and you need to get them some training so they can fix this pretty quickly as they'll be burning through data that you're paying for.

DMC to Sales
Now you know the team is going to speak to 180 decision makers you can start estimating your sales.

Let's assume your team are getting a 25% conversion (they sell your product to 1 in 4 of the decision makers they speak to) then you'll be gaining 45 sales each day.

Now remember the things we talked about before regarding the cost of your product etc. So if your product sells for a few pounds you'll probably reach that sort of conversion presuming you speak to the right people. But if your product sells for hundred's or even thousands of pounds then your conversion is more likely to be 10% (or 1 in 10) or less.

After a while you'll be able to establish a pattern of what happens on a daily, weekly and monthly basis.

This is when we move into the realms of MIS (Management Information Statistics)

This is the stuff that a Team Manager or Team Leader would provide to the Sales Manager/MD/FD.

This is pretty much where you take your KPI's and summarise it into a report. The Senior management won't necessarily want to know how you did it just the results of what you did and what that will mean for future business.

You have to get into the habit of keeping all these statistics up to date and be able to analise them so that you can look for any issues with the team.

It also means that over the space of 12 months you will be able to see any peaks and troughs for the team and then in the consequent months and years you will be able to prepare for them and act accordingly

Of course, you can always put in place a CRM system as I mentioned earlier.

As I mentioned, a CRM system can be very useful as your team grows and will be able to collate most of the facts and figures we've just talked about for you.

They can also be very good for keeping notes about customers – spending patterns and levels etc.

One other thing I feel I should mention that has been found to be very useful in the past is mystery calling.

Mystery calling is a great way to "test" your team once they're up and running. You customers may not tell you if they're not happy with your service or the way your people deal with calls – they'll just go to your competitor.

Using an independent company will give you at the very least an honest view of how your team is performing etc.

Mystery shopping is prevalent in the High Street today for shops, bars, restaurants and service stations. This allows precise top-down policy implementation and management to remote branches because head-office knows what the exact customer experience is and can act on that very quickly.

For many customers today the only human contact that they have with an organisation is via a phone.

My advice is put yourself in the shoes of your customer. Mystery Shopping does this and provides a very powerful feedback loop to management as it can focus on very specific issues.

Naïve managers think they know what the customer experience is just because the call-centre is located in the head-office. Likewise outsourcing call-centre activity poses an equal risk of poor customer service.

Mystery Shopping reduces this risk - Demitris Edwards, Vocall.

For more info on mystery shopping contact Demitris, on +44 (0)1242 690491, Demitris@vocallgroup.com or their website at www.vocallgroup.com

---

Section Five

Keeping them motivated

As with any sales team one of the biggest jobs/worries that the team manager has is keeping them motivated and focused on what they're there for.

In this section we are going to look at several topics, namely

- Environment
- Empowerment
- Incentives etc
- Appraisals
- PDP (Personal Development Plans)
- Training

Let's start at the top of the list with environment. I touched on this at the beginning of the book but it won't hurt to go over some of these things again as they are just as important as an ongoing issue as they are when you're setting up.

Which team do you think is going to perform the best, the team that works in a nice, clean, tidy office where everything works properly and how it's supposed to or the team that has to work in an office that's messy and half the equipment is broken or on it's way out? Doesn't take a lot of working out does it!

The better the environment the better the team will work, if they have the right equipment, that works when and how it should the better they will work.

It's quite important for an efficient, well performing team to not only start in a good, clean environment but to make sure it stays that way. Even if you have to assign members of the team the task of keeping it clean it's ultimately worth it.

Which brings me nicely on to empowerment. The easiest way for me to describe what this is, is that's it the ability to make the team feel that they belong and that it's, as such, their team.

If they take pride in the team and their performance then they will perform well.

It's always a good idea to let them all have a say in how the team runs – I don't mean make it a free for all, you still need to have a team manager, I mean the team manager should allow the rest of the team to give their input and ideas when things are discussed at meetings etc.

An empowered team will 9 times out of 10 perform better than one which isn't because they care what the team does and are more likely to meet the targets you set them.

Appraisals are another vital part of operating your team. You should set in place regular appraisal meetings with every team member right from the start.

Set action points and make sure everyone keeps to them.

A monthly one to one which includes time to complete an appraisal is normally enough if you also add in weekly coaching sessions with each team member.

An appraisal is used to make sure the agent is progressing not only how you want them to but also how they want to. It will form part of their personal development plan as it will show (hopefully) a natural progression in their role.

It's not that you want to create a team full of want to be managers, some of them genuinely won't have any desire to be a manager, but you still want to see them improving month on month and year on year. If they progress and get better then the company progresses and gets better, which ultimately means more sales and more revenue.

If you have a HR manger or similar then they will be more than capable of creating an appraisal document for you – with the help of the team manager – if not then you can find a perfectly good one by searching the internet.

You have to make sure that your team manager keeps on top of the appraisals because it holds the team together, not least because nobody wants to have a bad appraisal.

Whether you feel the need to have personal development plans is entirely up to you. Some would see them as a glorified appraisal, but others, myself included, see them as a way to not only give each agent something to aim for but also a means to measure each agents ability, skills and performance and to empower their performance.

Keeping your team with a cheery disposition can be an up hill struggle but it doesn't have to be. The incentives you offer your team for doing their job better can be a great performance booster, but you also have to work out what each team member likes and wants.

One of the best ways I've seen of getting to grips with this is to get each agent to fill in a questionnaire of their likes, hobbies, favorite drink, food etc. You can even go as far as to ask them specific questions such as if you could spend £25.00 what would you buy.

Then you have to look into when and how you offer the incentives.

The trick with sales people is this, they are obviously aiming to beat their target so that they get their bonuses but what they love to do is be the best in the team, by their very nature sales people want to be the best so they can show off. I appreciate this sounds a bit brash but that's how sales people are. I know when I was working on the floor selling it was a great feeling to be the one everyone wanted to be as good as.

You can use this attitude to your advantage by offering “on the spot” prizes and daily targets for a particular prize, it doesn’t really matter to the sales person what the prize is, they just want to be the one that wins it – it’s basically bragging rights.

I would advise that you look into the does and don’ts of this because the rules have changed over the last few years, gone are the days when you can give agents all sorts of stuff, now you have to be aware of the tax implications, so for your own sake check it out first.

The simplest things can have the greatest effect. To give you an example I’ve had a 48 seat call centre playing pass the parcel – if you get a sale you get to unwrap – and we had grown men and women getting excited over wining a bag of marbles, a little disturbing but it made a massive improvement to the sales figures.

Something else that has become more and more popular over the last couple of years is health and fitness for your team with companies engaging the services of personal trainers etc to keep the agents on their toes.

“A fit and healthy employee will be more productive and less likely to have days off sick. Research by the

CBI shows that the cost of staff absence costs the UK economy billions of pounds each year. Staff can be encouraged to fit in more exercise into their daily routines by walking to and from work, if staff catch the bus why not get off at an earlier stop and walk?

Lunch times provide a great opportunity to get some fresh air. As much as 250 calories can be burned off in a brisk 30 minute walk!

If staff are working in a seated position for long hours they should be encouraged to get up and do some simple stretches to help maintain flexibility and reduce muscle soreness. A small amount of time is required to perform these and the long term benefits are worth the investment.

Finally a regular intake of fruit will help to maintain blood sugar levels so staff won't feel tired and lethargic during mid morning and mid afternoon. Instead of buying cakes for staff why not allocate one day in the week where a variety of fruit is provided? This will help staff receive a good mix of nutrients, keeping them alert during the day and over the long term help to fight those potential colds that tend to be spread easily around the office!" – Dave Lewis, Calon Personal Training

For further information you can contact Dave at Calon Personal Training, www.calon-pt.co.uk

---

I have purposely left the issue of training to last in this section because it's probably the biggest subject and some would say one of the most important.

Training takes many forms, dependant on what your team is tasked to do. I would suggest that training sessions are delivered regularly so as to keep your team "on it's toes" as it were.

To expect anyone, no matter how experienced or tenacious, to keep motivated and performing at their best without any sort of training, motivation or incentive is, quite frankly, expecting a bit much.

In days gone by when I was running teams myself, we always had a mini training session at the start of the day or the beginning of the shift whichever was the most sensible.

If you remember when we talked about the set up process and we covered calling hours, I suggested that you pick a specific time of the week when you are going to gain the least response and use that time to more effect by having a training session then.

Most of the training sessions can and should be delivered by the team manager, they will after all know the team best and which skills need more work.

Training sessions should also be recorded in everyone's personal development plan, if you decide to use them, as a means not only to check that an agent has received certain training but also as a means to gauge their progress for appraisals etc.

With an outbound team the training sessions should be focused on the obvious topics, such as

- How to approach the call
- Features and benefits
- Selling techniques
- Open and closed questions
- Building a rapport
- Handling objections
- Getting past gatekeepers
- Closing techniques

Whereas if you are operating and inbound or customer service team, although some of these will still be relevant, such as building a rapport, handling objections and the like, you may also want to add in things like

- Listening skills
- Customer interaction

Whatever your team is tasked with doing for you one of the most import things you must train them on as much as possible is product knowledge.

All the skills I've just mentioned will mean absolutely nothing if they don't know what they're talking about. All the sales skills they may have will be a waste of time if when they get asked a product question they can't answer it!

They have to have all the skills we've just mentioned, they have to know what they're talking about and how to put that across to the customer in a clear and concise manner.

You will find that as you are dealing with people and all their funny little ways, that some agents will take in things better than others.

That's why I suggested that you record training sessions in each agents file, PDP or in your own files. So that when an agent says to you "I don't know how to do that" or "I've never been shown that" or any other such excuse then you can go back through your training files and check.

I promise you this will happen and if you have no record of who's had what training and when, then you don't have a leg to stand on. If you are at the disciplinary stage this sort of thing can be very useful.

Regular and relevant training is massively important to the success of your team, whatever they are doing for you. Make sure you implement a structured training program as soon as possible. It may seem a little over the top at the beginning but it will reap dividends in the long run.

Just to quickly talk about these things as regards using an outsourcer.

You can ask them when you meet with them about their training programs, do they have a training team or do the team leaders conduct the training.

Ask them if they run incentive schemes for agents and what sort of thing do they do.

You'll be able to see the environment when you visit them, but do ask to see the floor when it's operational and ask to speak to a couple of agents – they may not like the idea or even let you but the least it will do is show them you mean business and you know what you're looking for.

Section Six

Final thoughts

Ok, I guess we've covered pretty much all we need to cover without, hopefully, completely blowing your mind. I do appreciate that it's quite a lot to take in, but you have the book now so you can always go back through it or just read the section you need reminding on.

What I want to do is just give you a summary of the book, if you like as a quick reference guide.

- Decide why you want to use a telephone based team
  Remember there's lots of different reasons for using them.

- Work out your cost per seat right at the start
  Make sure you know what it is and set your targets accordingly

- Make sure you get decent equipment for them to use
  You don't have to spend a fortune, just make sure the equipment you get (phones, chairs etc) can cope with the workload.

- Create a good working environment.
  Remember, clean and tidy gives a much better result

- Set your team structure
  Have someone to run the day to day stuff

- Organise your calling hours
  There are times when you get a lower response rate, work out when they are and make sure the time is productive.

- Write your script and keep reviewing it.
  Write it, practice it, train with it and change bits if you need to.

- Organise enough qualified data
  You have to give the team a fighting chance so make sure the data you have them using is up to date and relevant

- Set targets (remember SMART)
  If you don't set them any targets what are they aiming for?

- Keep on top of your KPI's and MI
  Work out what you'll need to know and record it daily. You need to know at any given time

how your team is performing – and those you report to will also want to know.

- Implement a structured training program
  Put a program in place and make sure it is followed, keeping your team properly trained is vital

- Conduct regular appraisals
  Give the agents something to aim for and achieve, it will create a great mindset that will bring rewards.

- Implement an incentive/bonus program
  Again it will keep the team interested and focused, which is exactly what you want.

- Use spot prizes
  Make sure you have the impromptu stuff as well as the set program, it can give you a great boost on quiet days.

If you follow this book and it's content you will be able to set up and operate a telephone based operation, inbound or outbound, and make it successful.

The level of success you achieve is in your own hands and will depend largely on the amount of effort you put in and how much you get your team to do. But the basics are there.

Keep this guide to hand and refer to it regularly.

All that remains is for me to wish you the best of luck with your new venture, it will no doubt be both frustrating and rewarding but stick with it and the rewards will be yours.

SD - #0029 - 070726 - C0 - 197/132/3 - PB - 9781844267248 - Gloss Lamination